To: Ms. Luhrs,

Thank you for your support. ☺

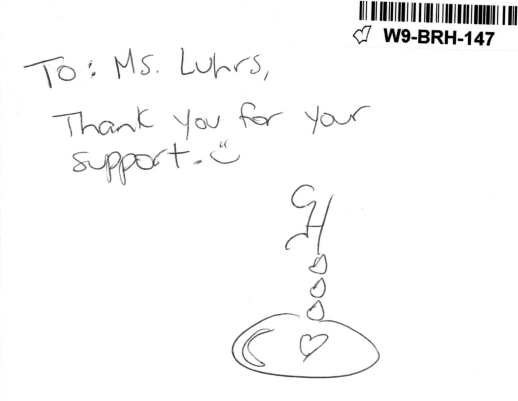

Ink Clots,
Tear Stains,
Blood on Cross
Where America finds true freedom again

By
Shameka Hamlet

iUniverse, Inc.
New York   Bloomington

Ink Clots, Tear Stains, Blood on Cross

iUniverse books may be ordered through booksellers or by contacting:

iUniverse
1663 Liberty Drive
Bloomington, IN 47403
www.iuniverse.com
1-800-Authors (1-800-288-4677)

Because of the dynamic nature of the Internet, any Web addresses or links contained in this book may have changed since publication and may no longer be valid. The views expressed in this work are solely those of the author and do not necessarily refl ect the views of the publisher, and the publisher hereby disclaims any responsibility for them.

ISBN: 978-0-595-52355-9 (pbk)
ISBN: 978-0-595-62409-6 (ebk)

Printed in the United States of America

iUniverse rev. date: 11/19/08

To Neesh- Maybe NOW you will read them. lol. 143

Acknowledgements

Thank you Nana, my favorite grandmother for believing in me enough to support me and encourage me throughout my entire life. I honestly don't know where I would be without you, and I love you.

Thank you Ma and Dad for birthing me into the world and the love that you have shown me through good times and bad. I love you and am thankful for you.

Danell and Neesh- big brother and little sister- we all went our separate ways, but you have a place in my heart that won't be taken away. I love you, and keep your heads up.

Thank you Rye Neck Union Free School District for 13 years of education and experiences that have played a huge part in who I am today.

Thank you Harrison Presbyterian Church for your support throughout the years and being a foundation for my relationship with God.

Thank you Nyack College for the best college experience I could've asked for, helping me to grow as a woman intellectually, socially, spiritually and physically. I owe you (literally... I have to pay off my college debt!)

Thank you MC2 and Pastor Peter Ahn for getting me out of my comfort zone, whether by getting me up on stage or giving me the chance to explore other states in the U.S.A. outside of the Northeast.

Thank you Los Angeles Dream Center for giving me the opportunity to serve others and be more optimistic about my life.

I have been thoroughly blessed to be a part of the huge impact that you are making throughout the world.

Thank you everyone who I have met and will meet along the way, and who I may never meet. You are a part of my life because you are reading this now...

Preface

As I was deciding to put my book of poetry together, I wondered: who would be the target audience, and who would take the time to read it? I feel that this book is more like a rhythmic diary than just a sequence of poems. Maybe I will leave a legacy the way that Ann Frank the Holocaust survivor did, or how Martin Luther King, Jr. the racial integration promoter did... maybe I will be like Jesus Christ, impacting everyone that He came in contact with. Instead of simply hoping that someone is intrigued by my private journal entries after I die, I figured that I should just go ahead and publish a book of poems taken from a collection that I have written throughout my preteen years and into my early twenties- definitely a radical journey.

I wonder if Shakespeare would have guessed that his plays would be read in literature classes and performed in Hollywood in the twenty-first century. Speaking of English, being grammatically correct ain't too important in poetry- I mean it is not too important. Sometimes you just have to flow as words come to mind, like a run-on sentence. Throughout this book will be an American Run-On, a poem that captures bits and pieces of the United States culture in post-modern lingo. As Americans, we are used to fast pace and quick fixes, running on and running out of breath, and our attention spans are limited just as yours probably is as you read this Preface. I usually do not read prefaces in books, so it's cool that you are reading mine right now.

Anyway, I won't deny that I have some American pride, but more important than that, I am a Christian, and I love Jesus. However, I do want to say something to non-Christians who are reading this: all of us are on a journey as people, whether it is mundane or adventurous. These poems are a reflection of my journey, and I do not want you to avoid reading it just because it may be labeled a "Christian" poetry book.

I think the title of this book, Ink Clots, Tear Stains, Blood on Cross can speak for itself, particularly after you finish reading the book. I wrote, I cried, I prayed. Just to be honest, I am getting bored writing this Preface (American attention span), so I am going to end it with these last few comments. I hope that everyone who reads the following pages of this book will step out of their comfort zones in one way or another, whether it is how you choose to view life or how you live life. I moved from a small, suburban, quiet town in New York to a huge, busy, gang infested city in California... sometimes we need to take risks to grow.

Whoever you are and wherever you are going, I love you, and God bless your life. You are not alone.

Poeticize for Christ,
Shameka Hamlet

"Being Human"

Human beings are interesting creatures. They don't communicate through barking, chirping, meowing, or mooing, but rather through words. Their words are suburban, urban, rural, grammatically correct and slang. Different languages, different cultures, different genetic make-ups. Meat eaters, chocolate lovers, vegans. Humans with five senses, yet sometimes can't make sense. Sixth sense- mind, thoughts, emotions. Similarly different.

Obesity, famine, cancer and cocaine

Three Colors, One Flag

They call it red, white, and blue. I call it Y-O-U

Blind to the beauty of a freedom passed due.

Red blood is shed in selfishness and pride

We have learned how to hate and put love aside.

White tissues to blot away and hide our tears

White man supposed to protect us from our sleepless fears.

The blues is the music that we often play

In a weird, twisted way, it brightens up our day,

Like the sun shining in a cloudless blue sky

An unquenchable thirst makes our insides dry.

With care-free authority, our "flag" sways in the wind

Unaware of the mess we Americans are in.

Heads are lowered in awe of the stripes and stars

But think about it...

Do they represent who you really are?

I love this country, the United States

May it find true freedom before it's too late.

Silent nights and stimulants for rotting brains

Copy Write Poem

I am trying not to make this poem a cliché
But something tells me it's going to come out that way
I can't find the words to make it completely my own
Every idea is stolen, so I'll leave those alone
Tapping my pencil as I tap into my heart
It's taking so long for this poem to start!

Okay, I've got it! I'll write nothing at all.
Pure originality is where I will fall.
Nope, I'm still not writing. I will not conform!
Poetry has become an uncomfortable norm.
I don't want to mess up "I" by stealing someone's style
Maybe I will let my right hand relax for a while.

All right, you caught me. I can't put this pencil down.
If I copy you, oh well. It's now my own sound.
This will not be my last, and it sure isn't my first
If you think this is bad, I have written worse
Sit tight and unwind as this poet keeps growing
The more you read on me, the more you'll start knowing.

Horse shoes, lucky seven, the American dream

Back in the Days

Back in the days, everything was all peaceful
Not worrin' 'bout the signs of evil
But now you gotta be on the prowl
Getting people to watch your back
Boom bang- that's the sound of cracklin' guns
Takin' the lives of very young

People hangin' 'round the streets
Smokin' crack and weed
Not giving anything 'bout people's needs
Taking 'way somebody's life with a gun or knife
Getting buried in the grave with what their lungs gave
People don't care 'bout nobody nowadays

You can't even walk out of your apartment door
Without thinking what these people have in store
You should just bring your own knife to save your own life
All you see in the city is a sign of no pity
Mostly all you hear in town are the loud gun sounds
Killing, hurting, making everyone mad
The anger grows quicker, thicker by the minute
Making everybody think about the good things we had
Back in the days

Behind a ladder, black cats, the number thirteen

Dear Mr. Shakespeare

To you, oh Poet, who wrote with "thees" and "thous"
There is something that I would like to say to you now.
Thank you for your English elegance and fame
I applaud you because I now love my last name.
I, too, am a poet, centuries after you;
"To be or not to be?" was a thought I had, too.
You are a reason why I exhaust my pen-
I guess you wrote with a feather and ink back then.
I may never compare to you, Mr. Shakespeare,
But I'd rather live for Heaven than be well-known here.
If it is God's will, I shall meet you, in time.
Till then, I call you my Great Grandfather of rhyme.

Praying hands, middle finger, a thousand rock bands

Can't You Tell?

My feelings are like Play-Doh, molded by a child.
Please don't push my buttons; I would rather not be dialed.
Hang up the phone, and put the Play-Doh in the jar
'Cause when I get pissed off again, a smile is pretty far.
Don't ask me why I'm angry; it will not make no sense.
You'd think there is a clearing, but the fog is pretty dense.
Taking a deep breath and praying may not do the trick,
But if I keep on living this way, I'll end up pretty sick.

"I hate that poser! Oh wait, I'm her biggest fan!"

So Long Secret

You don't see them 'cause they're my little secret

They beautify my face with transparency

And dry up with white like purity

I discovered them in infancy and have used them ever since

They're my companions in pain, joy, thirst, and when I reminisce

My eyes dread the vacancy of liquids so precious,

Finding their new home on my cheeks, chin, and neck.

In this temporary farewell, my eyes turn to a light reddish tint

Like white clouds suddenly smothered in blood

My secret responds to the depths of my soul

Tickling my face for an hour or so.

Italian one-o-one. Oh kiss me, I'm Irish!

Brain Crash

Getting pissed off with the nothingness feeling

I pray to God, but not facing the ceiling.

Looking down on myself, I feel so plain

Wanting to be free, but I can't break the chain.

My brain is held hostage by thoughts that control

They reach the peak before entering a hole.

I need to be whole, but I can't fill the void;

I would give it all up to be overjoyed.

I am sorry brain for filling you with trash,

But you will smile again before another crash.

Please do not curse. Instead, say the word "ish."

Procrastination

Putting off everything until the last minute,

Regretting that that homework didn't get finished.

Off to the mall instead of off to read books;

Catching up on soaps because you're officially hooked.

Ruining your future 'cause you're slacking off

Adult life is not going to be as soft.

Studying hard for about a half hour,

Then complaining that you just do not have the power.

Irked with yourself for postponing tasks

Never seems to motivate you to do what you're asked.

Afraid and stressed out that you will not succeed-

Tough-luck lazybones! Take care of your needs!

Instead of worrying about it, pick up the book and read!

Open your mind, instead of being so irked.

Now, to stop writing this poem and work! (Yeah right)

A liar, Savior, virgin, and prostitute

The 11th Day on a September

Today is the eleventh day of September

This day in two thousand one we will always remember.

Tuesday morning on a blue sunny day,

No one would've expected it to turn out so gray.

It still seems unreal and at the time so untrue,

People were suddenly supporting the red, white and blue.

A sense of patriotism filled the American air,

Feeling comfort in unity, although we were scared.

One tower, two towers, Pentagon and PA,

Were all bombed by terrorists on the very same day.

However, the Twin Towers no longer remain

The question is, will New York ever be the same?

With faith and hope the U.S. is strong;

United we stand- what could possibly go wrong?

"Don't these million dollar earrings make me look cute?"

Racism Sucks

The heart pounds hatred with a very loud beat;
Each day is a fresh day to spread the lack of love.
Why not show the world that you have some heat?
Might as well let them know what you're made of.
From triple K supporters to the fist of black pride-
So? We united after the Twin Towers fell,
It didn't get rid of the manmade borderlines.
Racists think they're right, but what do they know?
They are not the highest of the human race
Even though their ancestors may tell them so.
The truth is, they are the ones who pollute this place.
Racism is a war that builds up the hate,
Why can't racism just go away?

Larger boobs, bigger dick- can I say that out loud?

Immortal Heart

My flesh has surrendered to a battle not won
A strong passion murdered by the light of the Sun
In shame it dissipates, with wounds that fall;
Laid to rest underneath a deep purple shawl.
Dim memories are whispers of what it used to be:
Lust, obsession, fear, tension and idolatry.
There is but one part of it that still remains
The only part worthy to be cleansed of its stains
It beats like a drum in remembrance of Blood
That it once transported before the untimely Flood.
My heart's strength is grounded in a beauty unseen
A glory that is fitted for all eternity-
Love.

Jesus Christ! Damnit! Gosh darnit! Holy cow!

No More Yesterday

Inspired to write by the light of the sun

Warm winter breeze blows, rustling Christmas ornaments

It's rarely this warm this time of year in Northeastern America

The temperature must be pushing fifty, kind of chilly, but nice out

This is the last day of a short year, the sun will set soon

I don't think it will be bright enough for me to write by the light of
the moon

But that's okay. I will go back inside anyway.

Perhaps I'll watch Dick Clark let the ball drop

Maybe I will stare at my clock, anxiously awaiting 2005.

As with every other year that I have lived, there are ups and downs

Goods and bads

Greats and horrifyings

But the rustling of the wind tells me that tomorrow is not going to
be just

any other year

It is going to be the year.

The year of healings, true feelings, and lots of kneeling

The year of surrendering, rendering, and no more pretending

No more yesterday.

Can you hear the echoes of the year gone by?

Can you feel this breeze of hope that already brings trembling to
my bones?

The countdown has begun and will not stop at midnight.

Can you sense it?

Why is that grown man staring at that little girl?

Voice in a Box

Verbally I can't reach you so I'm writing this down

Since you won't listen to my voice, hear my pen sounds

My screams have been muted onto this sheet you now read

The proof of my tears is displayed by this ink that bleeds

You have talked over me and now I'm talking to you

In silence your eyes glide into this poem I drew

Will you listen this time?

If you read hard enough, you'll hear my voice

Crying out to you in rhyme 'cause I had no other choice

Will you return my tongue?

It seems that you have won the battle of talk

But sounds evaporate like the dust of sidewalk chalk

I am a woman.

I deserve respect, too.

Don't talk over me because you have the bigger voice.

Start this from the top and read it repeatedly

Then give me my tongue and lend your ear to me

"I will give you candy if you show me your world."

.

Broke 'n' Chokin'

Digging in my pockets and not finding a cent

"Don't worry about tomorrow," but I knew not what that meant

Trying to make rich the poorness of my heart,

But I'm so deep in debt that I don't know where to start.

This poem is a rhyme, so I won't make money there

My me is not magnetic, thus I'm feeling pretty bare.

Don't give me money, just give me a perfect life

And if that's asking for too much, I'll settle with a knife.

Digging in my pockets and not finding a cent.

Wish I knew where the screw all of my money went.

Church, dance clubs, graveyard, eighty story towers

New Orleans: Katrina's Corpses

Down here, the sun's breathing, not smothered by clouds
A long dark shadow casts for the humble and proud.
The eyes squint at the distant glamour of the streets
Beautified by a light that seems bittersweet
A stench of sorrow is spread by the wind of denial
The air so guilty, it will put all on trial.
Intoxication, altering mind, body and soul
A sense of loss makes it known that no one is whole
Cold bones, all alone with no hope in sight
Memories haunt, too nonchalant to put up a fight
Sorrowful is not a strong enough word
To describe everything that the eyes have heard
It's quicker to end than start all over again
A broken everything is difficult to mend.

Past, present, future. Second, minute, hour

When African Children Sing

Angelic voices of survivors sing amidst pain

Harmonic cries reach the skies saturated with rain

Dry, ashy hands clap in rhythm to a hopeful song

These hate-filled wars have gone on for way too long.

Innocence is on their tongues as they move to their beat;

African children can surely dance, even with blistered feet.

Sweat glistens their dark skin to substitute salty tears

It's amazing what a tune can do to dismantle fears.

Beauty from within is exposed during suffering

Love and hope can be found when African children sing.

Do you want fries with that? Mayo on the side

Blink Once

Steadily words fill this empty space

Lacking rhythm, but packed with emotions

Unexpressed desires, explained through the eyes

Blinking with weariness, questioning and disbelief

The eyes witness the poem unfold

Blinded by tears from stories untold

Beauty becomes treachery in broad daylight

The eyes observe loss with a desire to look away

Eyelids are a safe shelter from the cold, visible world

Protection from a reality that has become too painful

Eyes reopen.

Heart attack, drive-by shooting, my cell phone just died!

Love Above Lust

I watch you from a distance, gazing intensely
In hopes that you will be the one who notices me.
I wait for eye contact, but yours look away
Maybe you're taken, or maybe you're gay
Or could it be I'm too mysterious for you?
You'd be pleased to know that I see you that way too.
I spend a lot of time just thinking about your face.
The smoke of my lust could fog up this place
It's as if I have given up self-control
My wandering eyes and mind have rotted my soul...

...I have finally found someone who satisfies me
Who listens to my every complaint and plea
He drowns me in all of His love and affection
I can boast in His undivided attention
He's glorious, flawless and my eternal Love
He supplies me with Himself, which is more than enough
My left ring finger is empty, but my heart is occupied
Knowing that I have someone who gave me His life.
He captivated me with a cross and three nails
Allowing me to stand before Him, unveiled.

(Nothing satisfies like good, old American pride)

Violence

Pain felt in the heart emerges,
Loudly and strongly.
Anger smacks the enemy,
No mercy.
Invisible love, screaming to be seen-
In memory of peace.

Blonde, anorexic- how beautiful you are!

Hurricane Sin D.

She blows in your ear like a whore in high heels

Reminding you of what you thought you could no longer feel

She tickles your numb skin with her gentle touch

You stare into her eye and cannot get enough

Her danty, mini skirt floats above her knees

When she moves sexually, she stirs a summer breeze

Your sweat-soaked skin welcomes this unquenchable one,

Who with her beauty forms clouds to eclipse the sun

She seems to say "I love you" as she strokes your face

Your heart beats faster as her winds pick up pace.

She extends her hand to you, and says, "It is time."

You dig through your pockets, but cannot find a dime.

In anger and disgust, she throws you in a hole

Destroying all around you and rotting your soul

You are sore with regret and naked in your shame

For this hooker made you a victim to her last name:

Death.

Ignore that fat, black girl. She can't be a star

Painful Numbness

Fingernails dig into the center of the palms, red "U"s left over when the squeezing is done.

Calmness of the brain felt too heavily, aggravating the soul desperate for some type of overwhelming feeling. Good or bad, happy or sad, simply

dreading the in between.

Do I dig the nails back in to feel, or stay numb, my hands open?

Punching myself in the face, banging my fist on wood just so that I will cry.

Emotions

trapped

underneath numbness, tears dampening them, yet the numbness won't crack.

Anger not dealt with, rises and falls like a yo-yo, who's in control? Cry damnit, cry! Not

pain for pleasure, no, just any feeling is pleasurable.

Any feeling.

Am I sounding desperate? I am. I am as desperate as a Christian desperate for a touch from God- oh wait...that's me.

If you could screw one person, who would it be?

Give Me a Mic

My mouth opened wide, ready to free the scream

But my voice is softened, so the noise is just steam

Tangled in black confusion, drowned thoughts cry inside

My mask is well worn; a cracked, fragile disguise

Am I loud enough yet, or is my tone sounding mute?

This is me in my shyness, not trying to be cute.

I stand here alone, am I known in this place?

I have a picture of utter fear drawn on my face.

Cold hands pressed to my cheeks, the scream trapped within

I'm feeling like the loon that I've never been

So I will stand here longer just to prepare myself

For my scream that will shake even the silence of hell.

"Sinful" fantasies, HIV, MTV

Emotional Storm

The rain began to fall to the ground
Although it pounded, there wasn't a sound.
The cloud held on tight, but had to let go.
It just couldn't hold it back anymore
It filled up the land, ocean, and sea
Pouring out all of its sadness freely
The cumulus told it to wipe its eye
That there was no real reason to cry
The cloud just said, "You would not understand.
You are not the cloud that destroys the land."

Homeless people, middle class, and then Donald Trump

Restless Dream

A cross between New York and California
Nothing left to lose except security
I see snow on palm trees, warm weather in winter
I'm hallucinating in a desert with no water
Hills and woods surround me: Beverly Hills and Hollywood
On my own, I traveled to this twilight zone
Far, far away from home.
I miss you, Times Square, and I'm running out of time.
This dream has gone from nightmare to fantasy
And I know it will soon be my reality
I've been sleepwalking with adrenalin.
It's time to wake up, my eyes shut for too long.
Far, far away from home, but not alone
I'm in the hand of Him who made this
Twilight Zone.

Blak-Vu-nel-la (Black Vanilla)

Adj: to have the appearance of chocolate, but the flavor of vanilla; Oreo-like

Antonym: white chocolate

BlakVunella

I tuned my radio to ninety-two three,
A New York rock station that I found suddenly.
At the age of thirteen, I declared I was white,
Letting my blackness fly away like a kite.
Jealous of the girls with the flowing hair
Proud to be brown, but it got me nowhere.
I put on rags and attracted my own race
'Cause all they saw was the color of my face.
Maybe if I turned myself inside-out
I would've gotten my type of guy, no doubt.
Whatever, I am glad to be a black bella,
But don't forget, after black comes vanilla.

Yes, I'm serious...Oh no! You just got Punk'd!

Jerky Guys

You think that your actions are excusable
You walk around acting like you own her
She claims that her bruises are from falling down
Tears stream from her eyes when you're not around
She won't dare ask for help 'cause she's hooked on you
But you're flirting with other girls and her sister too
Just because your dad treated your mom like crap
Maybe you should have some balls and get over that
Your woman doesn't need your slaps, she needs your hugs
Instead of smothering her with hate, pour out your love
I don't speak from experience, only observation
But I don't want to live in a wife beater nation.

Pass me a beer. I can't take this anymore

You Are Not Alone

Do you ever feel life's coming to a halt?
When everything seems to be your fault
Your reason for living is because you were born
All your happiness is completely gone
You feel so depressed, you want to die
You cry all the time, but don't know why
Does any of this seem familiar to you?
There had to be a time when you felt it too
There is one fact that you should know
Your sadness does not have to grow
If you begin the search within your mind
Happiness is what you'll start to find

"Rationalizing Spirituality"

Theories. Conclusions. Case-closed. Regretting the past. Dreading the future. It's not easy being human. Too complex and confusing. Where is God? A question asked by doubters and believers alike. He's here, but where is here? Faith is like the new "F" word for a human who knows pain both physically and emotionally. Trying to hold on to that small piece of hope with hands that are becoming numb and tingling. Wanting to let go, but too scared of the unknown. God?

Nothing good on TV, and I'm super bored

Crazy Christians

Those crazy Christians think that they know it all
Predestined for Heaven after humanity's Fall
What makes them so sure that they are the "right" ones?
They would rather be holy and ruin our fun.
The church is full of people who want to connect to God
When the pastor makes a comment, they say "Amen" and nod-
What are they agreeing with?
It's like they're on a constant spiritual high,
With their hands lifted towards the sky, but I don't know why.
How can they sing songs to someone that they can't see?
How can they be joyful when the world has misery?
Why do they refuse to believe anything else as true?
Why do they pray so hard that their faces turn blue?
Who causes them to live lives that are out of this world?
Who causes them to dance, shout "Hallelujah" and do twirls?
Jesus Christ! What a bunch of crazy Christians.

You can buy this product for only 19.95!

The Knife of Satan

Embrace the snake, you idiotic one

Don't you realize your bad life has just begun?

Pick your head up off of that wooden floor.

Can't you see that God doesn't love you no more?

Bow down before your new master of life.

I am wearing a crown and armed with a knife.

You are nothing but scum, you filthy rag.

Yes, puppet, I own you. Here is my tag.

You're not the only one I claimed as my own-

Stop praying, you moron! Leave that God alone.

Ha ha! Yes! I want to kiss myself!

Another soul mine! Going straight to hell!

Aw, poor baby, just stop all those tears.

I've deceived you lovingly after all these years!

I think that Tupac and Elvis might still be alive.

Eye Twitch, Body Itch

Frantic panic invades my body caught off guard by boredom
A demon escaped and six more came back, took its place
Trying to remain calm, I attempt to ignore the storm inside me
But the anxiety that stiffens my body is craving to be seen.
I whisper "Jesus" with a dry tongue and sweaty palms
Fists wet and slippery, heart audible in silence
The hush of my exterior is the screaming of my soul.

Psychics, therapists, someone give me an answer...

It Hurts Again Today

How do you put your arm around a bony shoulder blade

Of a girl unable to eat because she's high on cocaine?

How do you tell a mother it will all be okay

When her baby girl got kidnapped and murdered today?

How do you comfort the one who does not want to be touched?

As he holds an empty beer can tight in his clutch?

For these people, there seems to be nothing to hold on to;

It's almost an insult to tell them, "God loves you."

We tell them not to ever ask God why

Don't question Him when one of their loved ones dies.

How come? Do you not see those eyes?

Puffy and red from an early good-bye.

I'm not about to spit out the Bible knowledge that I learned from above-

Instead, I want to wrap my arms around them and let them FEEL God's love.

Maybe I just need a hug from someone

Because I believe in Jesus, but sometimes I feel shunned.

God does not always answer our "whys", but I believe this:

That He will put His arm around your worn-out body, and carry you through it.

Twenty-five cents to see an exotic dancer

Liquid Wounds

Liquid streams from my eyes, but it's blood this time

Wounds, no longer scabs, drip out like red wine

Blinding self-pity, clogging up my throat

My unresolved resentment makes me bloat

My colors suit me well- black and more black

Surely this is a spiritual attack

Freedom is not supposed to look this way!

Joy mixed with bitterness comes out gray

You make me sick with your presence. Can't you tell?

Oh don't mind me. I am talking to myself

Go ahead and laugh, I think I will laugh too.

Because I know all of this sh*t is far from true. Ha. Ha. Ha. Ha.

College tuition, overseas wars, credit card debt

Halloween Teens

They walk around the streets on Friday night
They're way too big to play with kiddie toys.
Wand'rers they are, not knowing wrong from right.
Locked up inside does not bring them much joy

This is the generation that is lost
Their parents cannot see what they go through
Into a mind-numbing life they are tossed.
Fusing themselves with friends who have issues.

All that they need is to be shown real love
Darkness is bliss to disposable teens
'Cause in the light, they see what they're made of.
Thugs, punks, Goths, "normal ones" make up their scenes.

Lord, pump Your life into these living dead
'Cause Satan's not the one that they should wed.

Mr. President, I don't know if I can support you yet

Deep Shallows

I scream with a whisper and cry with dry eyes
Silence broken by the coma of my heart that's fried
The words "I love You" hide behind clenched teeth;
A prison that prevents my soul from going too deep
I escape Your kisses with my head humbly bowed
I want You to touch me, but I don't want it now
Like a bear in hibernation, I'm wide awake
Tiptoeing with comfort in the fiery lake.
If I formed a fist, would You still hold my hand?
Away I have led myself from the Promised Land.
I hear You call for me, but I changed my name
A thousand scapegoats with myself to blame.

Abortions, silenced voices, morals, censored words

Smile When You Are Ready

I only trust You when I know the answer

The hope and the wait makes my heart beat faster.

But when I find out that Your answer is no,

The doubt and the anger can't help but grow.

Why do You test me? You know I will fail

Taking in pain, but Your Word I exhale.

Happy when You satisfy, angry when You don't

Wanting You to free me, but feeling that You won't.

I'm caught up in the pissed off, screw the empty smile

You give me the world, but I only take a mile.

I know You say, "Uh oh. Here we go again.

I told her to trust me 'cause I am not pretend."

I can't see through the fog because it's pretty dark-

Shut up, Shameka Hamlet! Jesus has made His mark!

Stars and stripes, liberty, an eagle for our bird

Mud Cocoon

How many retreats do I need and sermons preached

To realize that You truly love me?

I sit here in defeat, unable to reminisce

Into all of Your provisions that have caused me bliss

Instead of indulging in sweet chocolate that grows from cocoa buds

I crack my face with pity-tears as I lie in the mud

The sunshine that once brought warmth and serenity

Is now solidifying the dirt that encamps around me

I long for a taste of that clear liquid treat

But dehydration keeps me from getting off of my feet

I'm tired, Abba, and the fountain is so near

Only a footstep away- won't You meet me here?

I know You are beckoning me to come and die

At this quencher on High that brings new life

May the heat fade soon as You cool me by the moon

In the midst of darkness I will break free from this mud cocoon.

This cream will clear your complexion and make you look hot

Spiritually Anorexic

Why do I reach for milk when I've tasted solid food?
Tolerating second best just because it tastes good.
I want a thirst like David, but I'm anorexic
Barely eating what's good for me is making me sick.
Genesis to Revelation, hungry for it all
Just like Adam and Eve in Eden before the Fall.
I'm starving with a plate of food in front of my mouth,
But I put it in a doggy bag and leave it out.
Jesus, take me by the hand and lead me to Your buffet
Because this anorexic can't keep living this way.

Turn on the news... another victim just got shot

Bitterness: A Step Backwards

The littlest things really piss me off
My interior hard, my outside soft.
Satan and I have me hooked on to hate
Wanting to be loved, but eaten as bait.
Babies aren't the only ones who need love;
Don't ignore me; I want to be thought of.
It's hard to receive love from One I can't see-
Is this selfishness that dwells inside of me?
How can I show love if I cannot receive?
This "body" of Christ, why should one believe?
Let's see how long I can go with this poem,
Trying to stop pain, but I feel so alone.

Bootleg, five finger discount, anti-piracy

Hollow Hallelujah

Overwhelmed by my stress and the love of God
These two aren't your average peas in a pod.
How do I fall prey to the rollercoaster rides?
Shouts of praise precede pitiful cries.
Lord, I love...what homework do I have to do?
You!...I really haven't got a clue.
God, You are...why you lookin' at me like that?
So good!...Want those eyes smashed out with a bat?
You're so worthy- what's that on my face?
Thank You for- man I look like such a disgrace.
Be with me, Lord...actually no don't bother
Unless I am ready to call You, Abba Father.
No, my Father, I need You desperately.
I will die if You hide Your face from me.
I can't depend on anyone other than You;
I will drop out of counseling and seek the Truth.
Lord, You are more than my more than enough
To Your hand I will find my own hand handcuffed.
In the pit of my stomach I feel a knot
Maybe it's me allowing myself to rot.
I believe, O Lord, that my hope is real
Temporary suffering is just how I deal.
As Christian sang, "Leave self-pity to die"
I want my identity in Jesus Christ...

Hatred, witchcraft, selfish ambition, jealousy

Untitled, Literally

The mirror has no reflection as it sits on an empty wall
Cracks appear from the false images portrayed overall
My palms are creaseless and my fingerprints are gone
Breathing is the only thing that keeps me going on.
Only A, B and C define me as what I appear to be
For being my natural self is not as easy as it may seem.

Standing underneath a light, I am not casting a shadow
Trip over a pile of rocks, but it ceases to cause a rattle.
The happy man on the moon is facing the other way
My skin begins to turn from brown to a pencil shade of gray.
Lightning refuses to strike me as I stand underneath a tree
The rain begins to fall, but deliberately misses me.

Miles away from reality, I sit on the bed alone
Hoping that my folded hands will reach my future Home
Writing on a piece of paper doesn't help because the ink will not come out
I guess that talking to God is what it's really all about.
Yeah, this life is fake and all the mess that it entails
Even if I get an F for self-worth here, in Heaven, I'll never fail..

Late night talk shows, infomercials, nose to chin yawn

Valley of Achor

Desperate for rain in a desert place- I thirst, You quench
Parched and almost strangling myself, but my body's drenched
I lick the tears that escape my eyes and caress my tongue;
Recalling in awe the waters of the Living One.
Sun darkening my skin, sin darkening my soul
There's a burning in my heart that slowly grows cold.
Sweat blurs my vision and I remember that sacred sound
Of weeping as the deepest parts of me were being drowned
Your softest touch brings vibrancy to hidden places
A sweetness so close to me that I can still taste it.
In this Valley of trouble, Your truth helps me to cope
Because I know that these crises are my door of hope.

"I have three hundred channels, but there's nothing on."

Don't Ever Act Too Hopeful

It's been a reality since ten trillion BC,

Yet all of it still seems confusing to me.

A voice forever silenced, the face no longer seen,

The only way to see it is in your own daydreams.

You did not say good-bye, or give your final hugs,

Unaware that this would happen to the one you loved.

Your body starts to shake, your eyes swell up with tears;

Comfort is uncomfortable, 'cause he's no longer here.

The corpse is still not moving, for he no longer breathes

His smile is permanently faded, for his heart no longer beats.

Gone forever is what hopeless pessimistic people say

The optimist feels well aware that we'll see him again someday...

Adam and Eve or Adam and Steve- who really cares?

Wordless Memory

I just had a thought, but I don't know what it was

My heart sped up, but in my mind, no words were spoken

I listen for a possible echo, but unheard sounds fade

As if drowned in the blood flow of excitement to my brain

My eyes search for the cause, but my surroundings give no hints

In anticipation I wait, with my fists clenched, staring

If it came once, it has to come again

Silence.

My heart returns to its slow, steadied pace

I inhale deeply the sleepy, scentless air, and close my weary eyes

In the maroon-tinted blackness, I stare at shining shadows

My skin tingles. It's coming back to me now

It was never a thought, but rather a presence felt

Touching my unseen soul, a wordless memory

If He came once, He has to come again.

And again. And again...

100% God and 100% Man

Jesus Christ is the man! He is also God. Just when we thought God couldn't possibly understand our dilemma, He came to earth in a human suit to experience firsthand what people experience. He came not only to sympathize with us, but to save us. He came to show us that though life is not always fair, God is just, and if we trust and believe in Him, our hope is eternal. He understands.

Just because he's dressed in drag, doesn't mean you should stare

Blindside

I want to go to the place where the sun never dies

Moving across waters, I'm sleepwalking in the sunrise

I am no longer held hostage by cute, boring love

Pitiful, so-called love with a teddy bear and fake hugs

I caught a glimpse of myself coming back to life

Holding hands with superman, I take a vow of silence

In awe, I watch as His mighty hands put back the stars

Through the Great Depression, He told me, "Time will change your heart."

When I remember being in the eye of the storm

I believe it was my Alibi who kept me calm.

This is not fleeting affections, this is a heart attack

You can hide it, but He'd be grieved to see your heart turn black

All of us swallow the tears that fall from our eyes

With compassion, He says, "On this shoulder, you may cry."

I have a headache because a thought crushed my mind

I think about His passion for me all the time

In silence, I daydream about a burning fire

I know that my blindside holds my deepest desire.

Freedom of expression, post modernism, anti-truth

Heart-broken Child

Happily ever after is what I am to be

Empathy for the little girl who's inside of me

Attempting to ignore her, but she will not stop crying;

Rapidly turning woman- growing up has been trying.

Tender soul, littered hole- is this why I am so weak?

Back away! Embrace me now! Balance is what I seek.

Referee pounds on the mat as he counts one, two, three.

Ol' enemy, bastard Satan, thinks he has the victory.

Killing him and my crappy past: the ultimate defeat

Every time I play it fair, he goes ahead and cheats.

"Nice job thinking negatively! Don't forget the guilt.

Clearly you can't break free from the shame you've slowly built."

Hearing this lie, I have a sudden urge to rise above

Influenced to please my Father, Whom I have grown to love.

Left punch, right kick mixed in with the blood of Christ

Ding dong the devil's dead- I praise Him who gives me life.

Retire to Florida, plastic surgery, keep your youth

Valentines

Valentine of mine, won't you take my hand?

Away I will lead you to the Promised Land.

Loveless you will not feel when I am with you

Every teardrop turns golden when you soak up Truth.

Nevermind the chocolates, gifts, and roses

Tenderly I'll hold you and call you chosen

Immortal our love will be, forevermore.

Not only your skin, but I'll touch your core

Enter into this romance I have for you

Since you know no one else can love you like I do.

Somewhere between New York City and L.A.

Surprise! I'm His Bride

I saw her over there washing Your blistered feet
With her long, flowing hair as You sat in Your seat
You gazed down at her with compassion on Your face
I cherish the times when You looked at me that way.
It is obvious, Jesus, that You are in love
Maybe our times with each other were not enough.
Your love card to me exceeds a million lines
You said that I was Your branch and You were my Vine
I anticipated Heaven- our Wedding Day
But since I've seen You with her, I have nothing to say.

My beloved, my beloved, hear me clearly
I love all of my children unconditionally.
Do not think for a moment that I love her more
You are speaking to the One who has named the stars
Your jealousy's uncalled for because you are Mine
I will unite you with Me when it is our time.
For now, I want you to bow down before Me
And accept the love that I have for you, humbly.
I adore your beauty because you are My own
In loneliness know you are never alone.

Beautiful Day

Today is a beautiful day because I have
God who listens when I sing
I am never alone now that He is with me
But He is omnipresent and He is with you.
I can't see Him, but I know
He is with me when I drink tea.
Also, He sees my actions;
With Him, there are no vacations.

Dia Bonita

Hoy es un día bonito porque tengo
El Dios quíen escucha cuando yo canto
Nunca estoy sóla ahora Él esta conmigo
Pero Él esta en todas partes y Él esta contigo.
Yo no lo veo, pero yo sé
Él esta conmigo cuando bebo té.
También, Él mira a mis acciónes;
Con Él, no hay vacacciónes.

Millions of people are dying and being born each day

Continuous Flame For God

Dear God, it is me, the one who's confused;

I sit here with dry eyes, but inside, I am bruised.

I do love You, **God**, so why don't I feel it?

Is my heart made of stone? If so God, please heal it.

The smoke is rising from a deceased flame-

Please God make the fire burn again?

Except this time, God, ignite it with gasoline,

Keep wind and water away so it will still gleam.

I have a cool, bitter chill blowing through my soul,

Oh God, without You, I cannot be whole!

This life is pitch black; let me see Your light NOW!

Make my image reflect Jesus, on the inside and out.

I need Faith, I want it, I must have it right away.

If I ever get wet, let me turn to You and pray.

I don't want to have doubts, anxiety or fear.

Dear God, let me realize that You are always near.

You are my Father, my Spiritual Friend,

So let me know that in my heart, but for now... Amen.

Air pollution, freak accidents, World War three

Whose Blood is This?

I've seen a place where darkness covers light
A person made holy who sins at night
Demons dance too close on God's own children
With a tempting rhythm, they lure us in.
It's contagious, almost pleasing at first;
Sipping a poison cup to quench our thirst.
I've seen the heart that will trade life for death...
Without even knowing it.
Captain of hell tells us to walk the plank of lies
The same plank we failed to remove from our own eyes.
We're not guilty, so why are we still chained?
Remember Jesus Christ, who died and rose again?
He rose again.

Astrology, theology, cosmetology

My Heart, Your Throne

I don't want another sermon or a song
I don't even want to be prayed for too long
Whether in solitude or a crowded room
I want to be completely absorbed in You
Staring into space, I am overcome by myself
My many idols are stacked high on a shelf
My soul is shaking, but my body is still
People are warmed by Your spirit, but I feel chills
I am painfully hungry, but my stomach won't growl
The aroma of my spirit is utterly foul
I shake with anxiety rather than God-fear
You try to speak to me, but I cover my ears.
I busy myself just enough to put You last
I hold on loosely while Yours is a steady grasp.
Drain me completely until I'm no more than dry bones
Then fill me up again and claim my heart's throne.

What idiot said that beauty comes from within?

Painful Rain

I can't tell the difference between blood and tear shed, except
One is crystal clear and the other one's red
The blood is visible pain while the tears express the same
A deep, merciless cut makes me cry in clear rain
Except I don't see no blood, just a blurry, fake reality
Blink once, the pain is gone, and in comes instant clarity.
Do you see my blood? Neither do I, but I see His though
Mingled beautifully with water as it expresses His sorrow.
Jesus.
I'm hurting again, but I see Your wounds clearer than mine
I look to Your cross, and...and it's restoration I find.
Where are my wounds? Oh, there they are
Hidden behind the Savior's scars.
Why do I still feel it then? Oh, I know why-
Because I as God's child am crucified with Christ.

In twenty-four hour casinos, we play to win

To Fight or Not to Fight

I have two options and two options alone
To fight with both hands or to complain and moan.
I can sit in defeat, or claim what is mine
Be a benchwarmer or join the battle line
For God's glory...
Will I let Satan and my flesh have the final say?
Or will I rest in God, and let Him have His way?
To fight or not to fight? That is the question
God does not condemn me to get my attention.
By His Holy Spirit, I am called to stand up
To persevere in reverence and not be backed up.
To live for my hope that is finalized and true
I know that is what my eternal Love would have me to do.

All-you-can-eat, feed the needy, finish what's on your plate

Relax and Die

My heart pounds like an angry drummer boy
Loud, rhythmic thumps in monotone
Seconds from death and days from the grave
Yet I will beat my body and make it my slave
Every moment counts when living for forever
Dying physically is no more than a scar
My feeble legs move forward at a surfer's pace
Though weak, I desire to finish this race
I hear the sound of my own breath growing thin
The heat of godlessness saturates my skin
Blood stains from Satan's rape ended in miscarriage
I have been united to Jesus Christ in marriage
Exhaling the familiar, I bid earth good-bye
Allowing myself to relax and die.

Fake emotions, empty smiles, and sex on the first date

The Feast

My mouth is watering, with saliva barely there;
Senses enticed by the feast that is being prepared.
Tangible hunger leaves the thirsty soul wanting more
A meal so satisfying that it will fill my core.
I wait expectantly, in utter desperation
The yearning I have can't compare to starvation.
Instead of a stomach growl, my heart is sighing,
Like an infant not fed, who will not stop crying.
The table is decorated with wine and bread;
Food for those who have been resurrected from the dead.
Delicacies that far exceed any buffet's worth
Are what await the heaven-bound, who leave this earth.

"I love the United States, and the stuff that pleases us

Abba Said

When I'm feeling stressed out about everything
And I sense that I'm flying on broken wings
In spite of dim corners, the Path is so bright
All because my Abba said, "My Yoke is light."
In the midst of praise songs, I wanted to complain
There were lies galore in this loaded brain.
As soon as I thought I could not win this fight,
My faithful Abba Father said, "My Yoke is light."
In the silence of my room, I was not at ease
Told Satan to flee, but he didn't hear me...
"My daughter, trust Me, for My ways are right.
Don't be weighed down by this world for My Yoke is light."

I have everything that I could ever want, why do I need Jesus?

Jehovah Part 1

I declare this day that pain will not seize my life

Not physical, mental, nor emotional strife

You told me today that You Are my Jehovah

Satan and his demons can just move their hell over

Through all of my years, You have carried me through

Forming me fearlessly in my mother's cramped womb

For too many years, I've let my hurts overcome

Crying my eyes out 'cause I thought life was done

You're my Tower of refuge, even at this hour

Why do I not feel in awe of Your power?

Lord! Lord! I can't live this way any more!

Why am I pushing You away from my core?!

Jesus come, Father come, Holy Spirit I'm dry

I'm bleeding so much numbness and I'm wailing inside

I'm so damn tired of putting others in Your place!

They can't compare to You, Jesus! They can't compare to Your grace!

I'm so sorry Lord that my emotions aren't strong

I'm sorry that my fear of man has been so prolonged.

Don't let me run away from the calling of death

Because Father, You are in control of my next breath

I will not allow these sinners to bring me down

They cannot rule my life for only You wear a crown!

Please let me inhale Your immeasurable peace

When I'm faced with trouble, may You say, "Trust Me."

Holy, Bible thumpers trying to steal the joy

Jehovah Part 2

Saliva drips out of the mouth, dries and whitens on the chin

Limbs trembling violently, unconsciously, uncontrollably

Eyes wide with fright, holding back tears

Fingertips force the arm to move forward, reaching desperately

Lightly tapped, not grasped. Palm of the hand sweating

Heart pounding, veins popping. Perseverance.

Stomach churning, feet tingling. Starvation.

Hand moves on top, stroking and caressing.

Heart stops and starts again, the mind silenced

The soul enters in. The flesh is hidden

Genesis to Revelation, hungry for it all.

Spirit unsatisfied. "More, Lord, more."

This is just a dream

This cannot be real

Blood dripping violently, unconsciously, uncontrollably

Everything becomes blurred, His beautiful face clear

I am in awe of I Am.

I wear a cross and a shirt that says, "Jesus is my Homeboy."

Twilight

Blessed Redeemer holds sunshine in His hands
Raising His arms to illuminate our darkness.
I'm unsure if the sun is rising or setting now
But, I know the One who gives and takes away
He inserts twilight between each day's extremities.
Amidst night and day, day and night, there's twilight;
An eerie peace despite what is on its way.
A separation of known and unknown,
But I think I'm okay with that
Because He who said, "Let there be light"
Lifted me out of that darkness between daylights.

Get the hell out of my face with your Christ religion

Eyes Owe You

Two spheres hand-crafted to display precision and grace
Pearls made of flesh they rest in a crevice on the face.
A rainbow coalition of browns, grays, greens and blues;
Alone they were created to identify hues.
Art and light are seen in extravagant uniqueness
Arousing all the senses that stir a sudden bliss
One quick blink, and a second of beauty will be missed.

The warmth of the sun is felt in bright yellows and gold
A faded blue and clear ice to acknowledge the cold
The details of earth hold a fraction of God's power
With a master paintbrush, He creates every hour.
His canvas is both loud and shy from morning till night
An echo of beauty passes between land and the sky.
Dreams capture the art of God's finger behind closed eyes.

In darkness, the mind's eye still remembers the color.
Vivid sleep is a photo in a frame of wonder.
But the eyes do not know about the beauty not seen;
The world is a whisper compared to eternity.
The perfect brushstrokes of Heaven are still in the works
And will be finished once Jesus Christ returns to earth
At that moment, creation will witness art's true worth.

I don't need you to tell me about the sin I'm in.

With My Head Lowered

I want to worship You so much longer than forever because

Forever doesn't seem like long enough.

Infinity to the infinitieth power of worshiping is only a speck of

The praise You are worthy of

I love You more than life.

You are my entire life and so far beyond my life.

I breathe in Your air, I'll die in Your arms

An unexplainable hunger that cannot be measured

Is what I have for You

You are Holy

You are Glorious

You arouse my senses with Your presence

You are the Great I AM

I love You

I love You

I love You

I love You

I love You

I love You

I love You.

What more do you need? What more do you want from me?

In the Mist of the Storm

Dancing to the rhythm of musical thunder
Sparks of lightning glisten with colorful wonder
Standing under black clouds, it's You and me now
The loud cries of the sky is the only sound.
I'm on a liquid dance floor, soaked to my skin
With such heavy winds, it's hard to breathe in,
But I do and I can taste You, sweeter than sweet.
There's nothing I want more than You this close to me.
By Your grace, You've shown me how to dance with You;
Keeping my feet steady, even when the winds blew.
As I follow Your footsteps, I dance gracefully,
In the midst of the storm, You drown me in peace.

G2G. TTYL. BRB.

Nothingness to Nothing Less

Your truth is more real than a physical thing
Your beauty, more genuine than a diamond ring.
How I love You, Lord, in good times and bad
I thank You that Your grace is not a passing fad.
You are unlike any other that I have seen,
As the grass becomes brownish, You remain green.
Sunshine plus sunshine can't compare to Your light.
Your beams are bright, but my eyes are opened wide.
People try to shrink You, but I know You're great
Too huge for me to put on an earthly plate.
Do not cease to be the Father of me
Although I struggle with sins of humanity.
In Your presence, my Lord, I will grow strong,
As I realize You were with me all along.

Slow down? Why? So you can tell me I'm going to hell?

Eyes Glazed, Body Raised

Deep peace floods the gap severed by chaotic sickness
Oozing to join the bitter separation of two worlds
Frozen sin now powerless to sustain a panicked soul
Now made whole by One called Holy.
Demon limping, paralyzed by the peace within me
I sit in a trance of transformational bliss
Too weak to even utter "Jesus" because He's all over me.

I don't want even a piece of what you're trying to sell.

Prayer

Prayer brings warm relief to the aching soul,
Like a blanket that shields from the bitter cold.
Breaths like vapor vanish into thick fog,
And crack the clouds with a sharp cry to God.
A deep conversation that shakes the sky;
Intimacy that lasts from morning till night.
Hearts being softened and lives being changed
All this for the glory of Jesus' Name.
The Holy Spirit intercedes with loud groans
To make known the words we can't say on our own.

Excuse me? Did you say free? Under what conditions?

You Are Healer

Yesterday, I was deaf, crippled and blind

Overcast by sadness and decaying inside

Under so much pressure that my heart felt weak

Agonizing bitterness made my soul reek

Rarely able to smile, barely able to stand

Entering a black hole that I could not comprehend

How is it now that I feel a sense of peace?

Entering God's presence has forced Satan to cease.

Awestruck by God's mercy without guilt or shame

Lifting up praise for the glory of His Name

Every wound and weakness has brought me to this hour

Released by the truth of Jesus' healing power.

Talk fast because I'm an American on a mission

Perfect, Priceless, Peacemaking, Pure Love

Surreal, priceless moments, hands full of emptiness

Alone with a whisper in my ear, and a warm embrace

I stand in my shame and kneel in humility

Dirt on my face, but I can feel You kissing me.

You took off my bandage and said, "Be healed in Jesus' Name."

Eyes bloodshot, in faith, I let go of my pain.

Gold flows like an ocean through the chambers of my heart

You suffocated time and space with how huge You are

Celebrate my celibacy, devoted to You

Never again will I deny Your love so true

Refiner's fire, unquenched by a storm of unbelief

I am free by the Blood of the Lamb for all eternity.

AndyArchieNydiaMikeMarkJuanArthurJasmineJeremySamArelisCh
ristopherThomasVinnyAlmaLouisKikiCherylBennyJordanJamieJoey
KimberlyChrisC.KimJ.J.Frankie MelanieSavannaChrisB.Scott

To Hot Topic 186

My heart was deprived, smothered by the dirt of this world

Lonely in a heart-shaped casket, it laid under earth.

The tear-streaked, white tombstone said: "Here lies a broken heart."

Sculpted in darkness, it was known as a work of art.

My heart was made alive by the precious touch of love,

A deep compassion for me that comes from God above.

I lost my heart to death in my confusion and shame,

But Jesus is the one who brought it to life again.

I used to have a heart that was blacker than burnt coal,

But my relationship with God has filled my dark hole.

In the short amount of time that I have worked with you

I have prayed to God for you out of my love for you.

I've knelt in anticipation at your heart's tombstone,

Letting my tears fall on it in hopes that you would know:

You are loved! You are loved! You are loved!

God will not force your heart to love him, but please know this:

Jesus Christ also died for Hot Topic one-eight-six.

My appointment is on six sixty sixth street, I can't be late"-

I Want to Be an Evangelist

My lips are parted just like the LORD's Red Sea
But my voice box is silent behind clenched teeth.
I feel my heart pounding as you walk away
I need to talk to you, but what should I say?
I smile and don't utter a single word,
Unable to act on my heart that is stirred-
I want to be an evangelist today
Reaching your dead spirit before it decays
Boldly, I will approach you, risking my pride
For the sake of your soul, I'll face homicide.
It is not like I have anything to lose
Giving you the option to deny or choose.
I chose Jesus, and in turn, denied myself,
So as to take my tongue and save you from hell...

"I know that what I have to say will be worth your wait.

Please give me these last ten lines, and I'll share with you my soul.

Jesus Christ is the one who has made my life whole.

In the busyness of life, we forget our spirit;

Tired, it cries "Wait a minute," but we barely hear it.

If we stop cheating our heart and play it fair,

We'd see that our American dream is just a nightmare.

When the clock stops ticking, and we exhale once more,

It will be too late for most to call Jesus "Savior."

God sent His Son and wouldn't have it any other way

Than to bring to Heaven those living in the U.S.A.

Wow, Lord, Wow

If I could just kiss You, my life would be complete,
The taste of Your love is sugary sweet
I don't have to see You to know that You rock,
Because when I am sick, You are my Doc.
Not only that, but You are my best Friend,
Giving me advice that I can comprehend.
You always prove Yourself realer than real,
For when I am sinful, Your grace I do feel.
When Satan starts to shake me, I try not to cry,
But when the fear starts to rise, I ask myself why.
Why am I beginning to doubt my Creator?
He is my here and now, not my there and later.
Why do You hold on to me, Father God?
Instead of a loud "Yes!" I give You a nod.
I think it is because You are so Awesome;
Magnificent, Beautiful, Holy, Famous One.
You reveal Yourself in incredible ways,
Presenting Yourself powerful- so why do I sway?
Bitterness, anxiety, lack of self-control,
These will never fill me- You will make me whole.
Oh my God, did I tell You that I love You?
You said in Your Word, "I make all things new."
I am beyond blessed to be Your saved one
I can't wait to see Your face when this earth life is done.
But while I'm still here, I am going to try,
To give You my body, my soul, my life.
Yes, I am aware that I will mess up lots
But now that I am Yours, I will never stop!
Hallelujah Lord, for Your mercy and grace,
How I desperately long to kiss Your face.
I am so excited to call You my Friend
Thank You for everything! In Jesus' Name, Amen.

"Closing"

If you have read through these poems and would like to receive Jesus Christ as your personal Savior and Lord, pray the below prayer, believing that He will hear you and answer.

God bless your journey.

Lord God, I have denied You and ignored You, but now I am ready to receive Jesus Christ as the Lord of my life. I am sorry for how I have grieved You. Thank You that the blood that You shed on the cross many years ago is enough to cover my sins. Please, Lord, show me what it means to live for You. Thank You that You have forgiven me, and now I can look forward to spending forever in Heaven with You. God, please bless my fellow Americans, and help them to know what it means to be free. In Jesus' Name I pray.
Amen.

Hallelujah! No matter how hard it gets, hang in there. God can meet all of your needs.

Author Bio

SHAMEKA HAMLET is a poet from a hamlet in Southeastern New York. From suicidal thoughts to spiritual ecstasies, Hamlet had to break free from her own destructive habits to embrace the liberty of being God's child. She hopes to keep turning the world upside down with whatever her future may hold.

Printed in the United States
130926LV00003B/359/P